Christmas in New England

CHRISTMAS
IN NEW ENGLAND

From World Book

World Book Encyclopedia, Inc.
a Scott Fetzer company
Chicago

Staff

Publisher
William H. Nault

Editorial

Editor-in-Chief
Robert O. Zeleny

Senior editor
Scott Thomas

Rights and permissions
Janet T. Peterson

Editorial assistant
Valerie Adams

Writer
Jo McLain

Art

Executive art director
William Hammond

Art director
Roberta Dimmer

Assistant art director
Joe Gound

Designer
Rosa Cabrera

Photography director
John S. Marshall

Photographs editor
Randi Sherman

Crafts artist
Alexandra Kalantzis

Product production

Executive director
Peter Mollman

Manufacturing
Joseph C. LaCount

Research and development
Henry Koval

Pre-press services
J. J. Stack

Production control
Janice M. Rossing

Film separations
Alfred J. Mozdzen

The editors wish to thank the many people who
took part in the development of this book.
Special appreciation goes to Lucy Smith, Douglas L.
Cooney, Annette Thomas, Edward Dodge,
Elizabeth Heistand, and Dorothy Hillman Thomas.

Contents

CHAPTER ONE

THE ONE I USED TO KNOW

CHRISTMAS IN NEW ENGLAND. THE WORDS CONJURE UP IMAGES MYSTERIOUSLY DEAR TO the American soul: the slow life of a quiet small town; white, clapboard churches crowned with defiant steeples; winter-bare elm trees arched over narrow lanes; the echo of laughter amid sleigh bells; and the exchange of seasonal greetings between neighborly folk as they pass up and down Main Street. The images are familiar to countless Americans who have never been to New England. Like Washington cutting down the cherry tree and Teddy Roosevelt walking softly but carrying a big stick, the images of a New England Christmas are part of our national identity—how we see ourselves. But unlike George's mythical cherry tree, Christmas in New England is firmly rooted in reality.

The small towns exist, snowbound in winter and little changed. Horses do, on occasion, still pull sleighs over the river and through the woods. Grandmothers continue to bake cookies, which are still left out on Christmas Eve to refresh Santa. And families continue to gather around the brilliant light of a tree to celebrate, in equal measure, the security and warmth of family cohesiveness and the birth of a Savior.

That this single aspect of American life remains little changed, relatively untouched by television, government, and computers, has more to do with the nature of Christmas than the nature of New England. New Englanders may typically take longer than Californians to leap into the future, but they are not as hidebound as so often portrayed. They were, after all, the first to thumb their noses at King George; the first to fire that shot heard round the world.

It is Christmas, not New England, that refuses to change. There seems to be a national consensus, unspoken but real, that Christmas must remain "just like the ones we used to know." Newfangled ideas do, of course, spring up from time to time; aluminum trees sprout in picture windows across the nation. But they are, soon enough, relegated to the attic, to remain an embarrassing reminder of the occasional lapse.

Eventually, we always go back to what we knew as children, what we want our children to know—and remember. And so, yearly, we recreate our own pasts: the remembered sense of anticipation; the sight of glittering trees, always different, but always, somehow, the same; the interwoven smells of evergreen and foods cooked only at this time of year; and the wondrous feeling of security that envelopes a warm house on a cold night. And so, generation after generation, certain notions about religion, family, and home are passed along. Children receive gifts, but more importantly, they receive memories, those early lessons cunningly taught and annually reinforced.

Christmas nostalgia. An 1885 etching.

But what about New England? Why is Christmas there so peculiarly appealing? There is, of course, the matter of snow. New Englanders, depending upon one's point of view, enjoy or endure a good deal of the stuff during the holidays. It usually arrives on schedule to bathe cities and countryside alike in the pristine white that is equally appropriate for Christmas and weddings. On Christmas morning, back alleys and abandoned junkers enjoy the same look of purity as churchyards.

Meanwhile in Mobile and Phoenix, families who may never see snow buy cotton batting to wrap around the base of their tree. And in Fresno and Bakersfield, the corners of patio doors get a shot of canned snow. We will have a white Christmas, no matter what the climate.

New England is simply the origin, the model. For people across the country, New England is where those Christmas memories, enacted year after year, first began. New Englanders left home for the rich farmlands of Ohio and Illinois and Iowa. They went in covered wagons to Oregon, and they sailed around the Horn to chase after gold in California. And they took Christmas, the Christmas they remembered from home, with them.

Winter Sports—Coasting in the Country by Granville Perkins. (From Harper's Weekly, *1877)*

Out on the prairie, a thousand miles from seawater, a family sits down to oyster stew on Christmas Eve. "It's an old family recipe. I have no idea how old." The same recipe is prepared on Christmas Eve back in Connecticut by a family of the same name.

A man in Dallas pays fifty dollars for a balsam tree. "I can't remember ever having any other kind." In New Hampshire, a man, who has no idea he has cousins in Texas, goes out into his woods to cut a tree: "A balsam, that's what we always have."

A lady in Portland, Oregon, spends the first Saturday of December searching for venison for her mincemeat pies. "Venison is very important. That's what makes it special." On the same Saturday, a woman in Portland, Maine, drives into the country. "I know a farmer who always saves venison for me. It's a secret, but it's the venison that makes my mincemeat different."

The entire Smith family of Albuquerque, New Mexico, strings popcorn and cranberries to hang on their tree. "Oh, I guess we've just always done it." Back east, on Nantucket, where cranberries grow wild, another Smith family sits around the kitchen table making garlands.

The customs and traditions of New England traveled across and up and down the continent. The image of a tall steeple, glimpsed through a clearing in the woods as the sleigh glides down a country lane, has passed into a living memory bank. And without ever seeing the original little town, families recreate it with cardboard houses grouped around a white, cardboard church, all nestled in cotton snow peopled with wax choir boys. We do it because we remember it from our childhoods; as our parents remembered it from theirs; as someone, way back, remembered walking, as a child, through the snowy streets of a New England town toward a clapboard church on Christmas Eve.

CHAPTER TWO

THE SPIRIT OF CHRISTMAS PAST

THE CHRISTMAS OF 1620 WAS A GRIM DAY OF WORK FOR THE COLONISTS AT PLYMOUTH. THE SMALL band of Pilgrims had landed in the New World only a month before, and the erection of winter shelters took precedence over any celebration. Besides, celebrations, especially for Christmas, were not highly regarded by the Puritan fathers. In England, Christmas had served as an excuse for drunken revels and pagan feasts. Religious observances had been elaborate and, in the opinion of the Puritans, altogether excessive. It all smacked of sin.

The prejudice against Christmas grew even stronger as more Puritans from England joined the Pilgrims in Massachusetts. By 1659, the colonial government officially banned the holiday:

> *Whosoever shall be found observing any such day as Christmas and the like, either by forbearing labor, feasting, or any other way upon such account as afore said, every such person so offending shall pay for each offense five shillings as a fine to the country.*

While these early settlers sternly ignored Christmas, they did create a feast day of their own: Thanksgiving. The first harvest in the New World was bountiful. In grateful celebration, they prepared a meal similar to what would become the traditional American holiday feast: wild turkey, fruits and vegetables, simple baked goods, and any food that could be gleaned from the land. With the harvest over and winter provisions stored, the people enjoyed songs, games, merriment, and the occasional exchange of gifts. This feast of thanksgiving became an annual event and, in the minds of the Puritan New Englanders, a replacement for Christmas.

Religious leaders of New England continued to denounce Christmas as a pagan festival and occasion for sin. Although the laws forbidding its observance were repealed around 1700, Christmas did not become a legal holiday in Massachusetts until 1856. Employers fully expected their employees to show up for work, and schools remained open on December 25. New Englanders of Puritan stock did not, in fact, wholeheartedly enter into holiday celebrations until quite late in the nineteenth century. But people of other backgrounds and faiths were settling into the colonies in ever increasing numbers. Immigrants from Germany, Holland, Scandinavia, and Ireland, as well as England, eventually ignored the Puritan restrictions and celebrated Christmas as they had in their homelands.

Church services varied from the elaborate rites of the Anglican and Roman Catholic churches to simple, quiet Protestant services in areas

New England life during the Revolutionary War was centered in the traditions of family, hearth, and home.

that allowed more freedom of worship. In Rhode Island, for example, settlers who had followed Roger Williams in an effort to escape stifling Puritan laws were free to found their own churches and to continue traditional Christmas observances.

German settlers strongly influenced the development of American Christmas customs. Their Kriss Kringle went through several transformations to become our Santa Claus. From German immigrants, New Englanders adopted the now-traditional Christmas tree. And a German military regiment contributed to one of the most famous Christmases in American history.

During the Revolutionary War, paid Hessian troops came to the colonies to fight on the side of the British. One such unit was fighting against George Washington's troops in the winter of 1776. The German soldiers held their traditional Christmas celebration directly across the Delaware River from Washington's encampment. The festivities lasted long into the night. As the soldiers slept off the effects of too much merriment, Washington took advantage of the situation, crossed the Delaware, and won one of the most crucial victories of the war.

The Dutch in the New World continued to celebrate St. Nicholas' Day on December 6. This custom eventually died out as the more popular

*Preparing Christmas
Greens by T. De Thulstrup
(From* Harper's Weekly,
December 25, 1880)

December 25 date took over, but St. Nicholas remained, eventually to be absorbed into our own Santa Claus.

Traditional Irish customs, some based on folklore, others on superstition, found their way to New England as well. The Christmas wreath is an old Roman custom, introduced to this country by Irish immigrants. The New England tradition of placing candles in the windows at Christmastime is also based on Irish practice. Superstitions of ghosts and spirits, purification rituals, and the like have abounded in Ireland for centuries, and settlers of Irish ancestry added this rich heritage to the growing mixture of Christmas lore that would characterize the New England holiday.

As anti-Christmas sentiments slowly disappeared and imported Old World traditions were adopted, the New England, and American, Christmas acquired its unique character. Religious and nonreligious elements merged, but very carefully. Christmas in New England was first, and foremost, the celebration of the birth of Christ, a religious holiday. But with the rise of a large middle class in the nineteenth century, the giving and receiving of gifts came to be an important part of Christmas in America. The Victorian era New Englanders, however, did not forget the lessons of the Puritans, and the increasingly lavish exchange of gifts, so peculiar to America, was bathed in a philosophy of charity and good will that has come down to us as the "Christmas Spirit."

This spirit of giving and of charity was first popularized by Charles Dickens in his classic *A Christmas Carol*, published in 1843. The book

The overwhelming popularity of Dickens gave rise to commercial art that evoked the same feelings of peace and good will.

Santa Claus has changed considerably over the years. Here the jolly gentleman, much thinner and in blue, carries a tree for the family he will visit next.

expressed what Dickens called the "carol philosophy." Christmas is a time for giving, not only of material things but of the self; it is the one time of the year when people place the interest of others before their own concerns. The stingy Scrooge, haunted by ghosts until he gives in to the true spirit of Christmas, is an example and warning to us all.

Dickens wrote a new Christmas novel or story nearly every year between 1843 and 1867. Although *A Christmas Carol* is certainly the best and most popular of these works, all were well-received and widely read in America and especially in New England. Each of these tales pushed the carol philosophy, and Dickens, himself, became an international symbol of Christmas. At his death in 1870, children in London asked if Father Christmas would die as well.

It is difficult today to fully understand the popularity that Dickens enjoyed during his lifetime. In our society, perhaps only actors and musicians receive the same adulation. All of Dickens' novels were initially published in installments, leaving the readers hanging, waiting breathlessly for the next episode. In 1841, the suspense over the fate of Little Nell in *The Old Curiosity Shop* became something of a national phenomenon in this country as well as in England. On the day that the ship carrying the magazines revealing Little Nell's death sailed into Boston Harbor, the docks were mobbed. People screamed at the passengers on deck: "Is Little Nell alive?" When it came back that she had indeed succumbed, grown men collapsed in sobs. No novelist before or since has held such power over his readers.

The newly affluent middle class, for whom Dickens primarily wrote, was deeply touched and influenced by the new spirit of Christmas that the author promoted. More than any other single element, Dickens' books were responsible for the intense interest in creating and reviving Christmas customs that was shown in Victorian England and America. Dickens had taken the morality and values of the church and applied them to everyday life. He gave the people of the time just the right mixture of ingredients for the satisfaction of both body and soul. The Victorians took it all to heart and created the Christmas of modern nostalgia. The giving of gifts, as tokens of charity and good will, proliferated. What began with an orange and a bit of hard candy in a child's stocking spread—to the school, the church, the clubroom. Everyone was remembered, if not with a personal gift, then at least with a tip or a card. And for good or bad, Christmas in New England, as in all of America, was forever changed.

New Englanders under the spell of Victorian Christmas magic forgot their prejudices against such pagan customs as mince pie, mumming, and decorating the house with boughs of evergreens. The Christmas tree became an ornate work of art during this time. Holiday celebration was adapted to the climate of New England, and Christmas became forever linked with cold and snow. The hardships of such a climate were lost in visions of sleigh rides and skating parties.

The traditional image of a New England country Christmas, little changed in over two hundred years, survives in rural Vermont.

Santa Claus also appeared, taking on his familiar proportions with the publication of *A Visit from St. Nicholas* in 1848 and the appearance of Thomas Nast woodcut in *Harper's Weekly*, beginning in 1863. The new personification of Father Christmas combined charitable gift giving with material comfort and shrewd merchandising.

Well-to-do Victorians, remembering Dickens' message of charity toward those less fortunate, prepared Christmas baskets of food and clothing for the poor. The benefits obtained by the givers, in terms of satisfaction and peace of mind, were as important as the aid received.

All negative aspects of the holiday were abandoned. No longer did children have to fear a switch in their Christmas stocking. Ghosts and evil spirits were banished by ritual, or they simply dropped out of most observances altogether. The work ethic that formed a part of this country's heritage from the Puritans to the Industrial Revolution was suspended for a short time each year. The magic of a winter wonderland and the mystery of a holy birth superseded it.

And so the nostalgic New England Christmas—the Christmas just like the ones we used to know—came into being. Progress has brought many changes, certainly. And yet modern Americans continue in the established traditions, and New England, most resistant to change, provides the model.

CHAPTER THREE

'TIS THE SEASON

CHRISTMAS IN NEW ENGLAND SURVIVED THE STERN DISAPPROVAL OF THOSE PURITANS SO worried over excess and sin. But today's "season" is far different from the ones fa la la'ed over in the old Welsh carol. In typical American fashion, Christmas has, during the 350 years of its evolvement in the New World, grown to a size unimagined by even our jolly Victorian ancestors. The "season" has grown into "the holidays," that almost continuous round of good cheer from the fourth Thursday in November to New Year's Day. Ironically, Thanksgiving, created to replace Christmas, has been nearly swallowed by it and has, in the twentieth century, become something of a seasonal kickoff. The "holidays" now seem to begin on Thanksgiving morning with a flurry of Santa parades and the enticing smells of rich cooking. Barely has the turkey been demolished when merchants, eager to attract shoppers, decorate their stores and fill the air with Christmas carols. Children begin wish lists before the first of December, and parents groan over the thought of paying for it all. But with the first snow, memories of childhood Christmases creep back, and all the grasping commercialism is mysteriously colored in Dickens' simple, nostalgic philosophy of charity and good will to all.

The Christmas season in the Christian church begins with the first Sunday of Advent (the Sunday nearest November 30). The Advent season includes the four Sundays before Christmas and is a time of spiritual preparation and anticipation of the birth of Christ. Many families have adopted the German/Austrian custom of the Advent wreath. A circle of greens containing four candles of progressively lighter purple (to symbolize the approaching Nativity) is placed prominently in the home. The first week, the darkest colored candle is lighted, then an additional candle in each successive week. Handmade or purchased Advent calendars, with one small door or window to be opened for each day of December until Christmas, add to the anticipation.

Christmas greenery appears on the streets and housefronts throughout New England. Volunteer fire departments scale ladders leaned against lampposts or balance on whatever equipment they have available in order to wind roping and ribbon up and down Main Street. Completely decorated miniature trees can be found sprouting atop poles in at least one Massachusetts town. Country inns, in anticipation of the holiday tourist trade, nail evergreens to their doors and hope for snow.

Traditional Christmas wreaths with a large red bow and perhaps a pine cone or two stand out against the green or black doors of white

Colonial houses and churches. Candles in pewter sticks are to be found in every window of many homes. Bells, evergreen roping, chestnuts, and holly decorate railing, fences, and lamp standards.

Store window decorations may be New England practical and subdued, allowing nature's own decoration, hoarfrost, to etch delicate webs in the corners along white window mullions; or they may show a "citified" flair for the elaborate verging on gaudy. In larger cities, huge decorated trees grow out of store marquees. But smaller towns still erect the tree on the town square. The community Christmas tree, decorated by the entire town, has been popular since the first appeared in New England, on Boston Common in 1914.

Soon after Thanksgiving the season begins in earnest at home. Decorations stored in dry attics and cool cellars are brought out and dusted off. It may be early, but there is so much to be done. Recipes are examined for those ingredients purchased only at Christmastime: citron, candied fruits, walnuts, pecans, fresh oysters, suet. The card list is found, after no little effort, buried under canceled checks and old report cards in a desk drawer. Christmas cards have, in the last century, become as traditionally a part of the holiday celebration as the Currier and Ives New England snow scenes they so often depict. The sight of Mother at her desk diligently signing cards and penning notes to rarely seen friends and relatives is a quiet, but sure, sign that the season has arrived.

The Christmas card originated in Victorian England. Social historians suggest that the practice began with Christmas letters to home written by boys in boarding schools. These were composed on heavy paper stock supplied by the headmaster and decorated with seasonal borders. Parents, delighted with the messages from their sons, soon emulated them. Printers, realizing the potential, began manufacturing cards specifically for the Christmas market. During the 1840s, painted cards began to appear. Looking very much like the then new and popular Valentine card, these were often three-dimensional and dressed with tissue paper honeycombs. In the thirty years that followed, English cards included small booklets, cutouts, and other ingenious forms.

The Christmas card was introduced to America by the Marcus card company and became popular immediately. A German immigrant named Louis Prang, who operated a small printing business in Roxbury, Massachusetts, produced, in 1874, the first of what would become a remarkable line of Christmas cards. The Prang card was intricately detailed and printed in as many as 20 colors; each card, therefore, went through the press as many as 20 times. Prang's extraordinary work was soon recognized, and by 1881, he was manufacturing over 5 million cards each season. Design competitions were organized with well-known artists as judges, for example, Louis Comfort Tiffany. The first

Louis Prang's tribute to homemade Christmas fun mirrored the spirit of the times. The Prang card set standards for design and printing quality that have rarely been equaled.

year's contest brought in more than 600 entries, and the money awarded winners totalled over $3,000.

Cheap competition, however, soon invaded the market. Mass-produced cards, some imported, could be sold at cheaper prices. The overall quality of the average card deteriorated, and the importance of art and craftsmanship dwindled in the mind of the average consumer. Prang, angry at the trend and unwilling to lower his standards, went out of the Christmas card business altogether.

Modern cards offer a choice ranging from the sacred to the whimsical, ornate or starkly simple. Competition among card manufacturers is intense. Billions of dollars are spent every year on cards and postage. In recent years, American preference has been for nostalgic scenes, religious motifs, and handmade or "country crafted" cards, indicating a return to a tradition that was never abandoned by most New Englanders.

Christmas is in large part a children's holiday, and life at school, Sunday school, and scout meetings centers around singing, programs, "pieces" to be memorized, and gift making and giving. Allowance, paper-route, and baby-sitting money is hoarded in the weeks before Christmas for presents for Mother, Dad, Grandma, and Grandpa. In New England, the snow is usually deep by the beginning of December, and sledding, tobogganing, skiing, and snowball fights fill Saturdays and those increasingly dark evenings between school and suppertime. Ice is thick on many ponds and lakes, and skaters in pairs or groups race and gather for informal hockey games.

Christmas cards and novelties have developed into a thriving industry. Modern well-wishers can be overwhelmed by the selection.

19

The annual search for a Christmas tree has changed little in New England. As illustrated above, small forests have, for over a century, been springing up on empty city lots. And in the country, farmers still exchange runners for wheels on their spring wagons before setting out in search of the perfect tree.

In northern Vermont, New Hampshire, and in Maine, some towns and farms are practically snowbound by Christmas. The snowmobile gives some access, but older residents prefer skis, snowshoes, or horse-drawn sleighs when the automobile is stopped. Everyone has a story about the *big* snow or the Christmas that almost wasn't. Grandfathers have, for generations, spelled yarns about the winters of their youth: how as boys they climbed out upstairs windows onto the snow and then walked miles to school using the tops of high fences as their only guide. Snows are never like they were back then.

These are the days for scouting nearby stands of evergreens, searching for the perfect tree. The less fortunate city dweller must choose his tree from a crowded lot, but the rural New Englander selects his as it grows. With quiet pleasure, the most likely candidate is singled out, felled expertly, and hauled home by sled, sleigh, or truck. Then it is tipped against the wall of the barn or shed to stand in the crisp air until the week before Christmas.

Meanwhile, the cooks of the family are busy indoors. Fruitcakes *must* be baked just after Thanksgiving in order to be properly aged by Christmas. Mincemeat, for which the family recipe is passed from generation to generation and closely guarded from the prying eyes of nosey neighbors, must also be aged properly. So the chopping, mixing, and packing in jars is done early in December. The baking then begins, to continue with little interruption until Christmas morning.

From the time of the earliest Christmas trees, food and edible ornaments of all kinds have been hung from the branches. The first cookies of the season are often designated as ornaments. Bread dough is also fashioned into whimsical shapes and, along with candy canes far too old to still be edible, hung on the tree to cover bare spots.

Extra baked goods are prepared as gifts for relatives and friends or to be distributed in baskets to the poor. The type and number of the treats varies with the background of the cook. Lebkuchen from Germany, ginger-molasses Moravian cookies, English deep-dish apple pie (in addition to the traditional mince pie), and breads from the Scandinavian countries have all become part of the Christmas menu in various areas of New England.

Sugar cookie dough is chilled, rolled into a thin sheet, then cut into shapes with tin cookie cutters. Grandmother, whose own mother may have used the same cutters, remembers when she was the little one standing on a kitchen chair trying to "help" cut out the cookies. And as she works, she passes on stories about funny old Aunt Kate and Grandpa Carter's beard, which looked just like Santa's. Extra tin men become toys for little Billy, who toddles happily underfoot. As stars, bells, and Santas come out of the oven a golden-brown, the children watch in hope that a camel will suffer a broken neck or a snowman will accidentally fracture a hip. It's such a long wait until Christmas Eve.

Christmas Eve in turn-of-the-century Boston. Late shoppers head home via streetcar or sleigh, loaded with presents or with a tree tucked under one arm.

The next day, the cooled cookies are iced and decorated. Colored sugar makes Santa's suit and covers green trees. Ornaments and sprinkles are added, sometimes a little unsteadily by the youngest decorators. Many hands, young and old, take part in the process, if only to judge the finished products before they are packed away between layers of waxed paper.

Candy making is also an important part of Christmas preparations. The sugarplums that caused visions to dance in the heads of children are made of tiny fruits covered with a crystallized candy coating. (The term has also been applied to any filled bon-bon.) Homemade peanut brittle is rolled out on a greased table or marble slab in the cool cellar, allowed to harden, then broken into small pieces. Other favorites include divinity, a relatively simple recipe, but one that requires considerable time and patience, and rich, English toffee, which only comes out right when made on those dry, cold nights before Christmas.

In other parts of the house, as well as in the barn or woodshed for those hardy enough to withstand the cold, craftsmen of all ages are working on handmade Christmas decorations and gifts. This type of work is a New England tradition that has recently taken hold in other areas of the country as well. Handcrafted ornaments and gifts are, in fact, in such demand that cottage industries and artisans's shops throughout New England are thriving, their profits enhanced by the Christmas trade.

Handmade decorations for the house and tree may be simple or

Top. *Baking cookies is a family project. Each child adds a personal touch, down to the fingerprints.*

Left. *Even the youngest try to wrap a special gift, the better to keep Christmas secrets.*

23

intricate, but they serve as a delightful excuse for a full family project: popcorn and cranberries are, of course, newly strung every year for the tree; and perhaps a new star is needed for the top; walnut shells, left over from fall hulling, are drilled for a hook and filled with moss and a tiny Jesus in the manger; delicate snowflakes, tatted by Grandmother, are marvels of intricacy; pine cones find their way into wreaths, pine cone trees, arrangements on the table and mantle, or are simply hung from the pull string of a window shade; nativity scenes, ranging from miniature to life size, are carved for both the home and the community; candles made from wax laboriously rendered from bayberries fill the house with a scent unique to the Northeast. The imagination and patience required for these projects are indications of the tenacity of the New England temperament.

Wood is a popular material for crafts and gifts in New England. Abundant stands of timber are filled with maple, walnut, hickory, and oak trees. Carving, whittling, and carpentry are still common, especially in rural areas, where farmers have time on their hands in winter, and in coastal towns, where shipbuilders and seamen predominate. Gifts, particularly for children, are often made by hand and in rich hardwoods. On Christmas morning, children in rural New England may wake up to find gifts that would be considered extraordinary luxuries in the city: building blocks made entirely of hand-rubbed walnut; Lincoln logs, all hand-turned, packed in a chest made of quartersawed oak; a store-bought doll, but outfitted with a wardrobe, sewn by Mother from old dresses and suits, and a trunk and doll bed, lovingly crafted by Father or Brother from native hardwoods; train sets, also store-bought, but layed on a table made by Dad, complete with miniature towns, water towers, and trestles. Mother may discover a new Hitchcock-type fancy chair, crafted entirely in bird's-eye maple. Boxes, shelves and brackets, toys, puzzles, bowls, and utensils are all turned out from home workshops to be placed under the tree. The tradition spans hundreds of years and continues as skills and tools are passed along to the next generation.

The custom of gift giving is an ancient one, extending at least as far back as pre-Christian Rome. In those days, gifts were given to celebrate the new year. Money boxes that had been used for savings all year were emptied and the contents used to buy gifts. In a similar fashion, churches through the ages have emptied their alms boxes after the Christmas giving season and have distributed money and food to the needy.

Gifts have always been used as rewards for good behavior in children. The reverse, of course, is also true. Bad children either receive nothing or a gift symbolic of punishment. In Germany and Austria, St. Nicholas is accompanied by a wicked-looking assistant. The holy bishop will distribute gifts to good children, but those whose behavior has been less than perfect will be faced with St. Nich's nasty henchman.

*During many a holiday season, Saturday skaters have met
under the old bridge at Worcester, Massachusetts.*

Responding to Santa's questions on deportment requires serious consideration.

Fortunately, St. Nicholas always intercedes on the child's behalf, evoking solemn promises for improvement.

Our own Santa Claus, lacking a henchman, is forced into double duty. A pre-Christmas visit to Santa Claus is incomplete without a grave inquiry into Susan's or Johnny's behavior: "And you have been a good little boy?" Grandfathers, mysteriously, seem to have Santa's ear and, with great relish, issue dire warnings: "You'd better be good, kiddo, or you'll find, as I once did, coal and a hickory switch in your stocking!" Although Johnny may never have layed eyes on a piece of

Frosty, the Snowman, a native New Englander, usually manages to make it home for the holidays.

coal or a real switch, the tone in Grandpa's voice, and the betrayal of his own misspent youth, are just enough to fill a little head with dark visions of sooty disappointment on Christmas morning. And so, Brussels sprouts are consumed, at least through the weeks of December.

Some gifts, of course, must be purchased, and New England abounds with the small, unique specialty shop, which provide items rarely seen elsewhere: colonial antiques, scrimshaw, tins of maple syrup and comb honey, woolen yard goods, ship models, goose down for pillows, comforters, and ski parkas. But for the average rural or village dweller, one shopping trip to a larger city—Portland, Manchester, Providence, Hartford, or even Boston—may be a necessary, and exciting, part of the holiday season. Christmas crowds, noise, hubbub, and exhaustion are all a familiar part of the metropolitan shopping process. A day spent in one of the old, downtown department stores—visiting Santa, seeing the toy department, lunching in the tearoom, admiring the store windows

Community, school, or church groups each present their own interpretation of the Christmas story in dramatic or musical productions.

and decorations, fighting for a clerk—may be as much a part of the season as hunting for a tree.

The New England city is filled with history, color, and pageantry that add to the pleasure of a holiday trip. No other area offers the same combination of these extraordinary shopping and cultural activities. The Christmas season in Boston includes special performances by the Symphony, the "Pops," cantatas offered by both professional and community groups, ballets such as the *Nutcracker*, Christmas theater performances, holiday shows at art museums, and community sings. Smaller cities have colonial and maritime historical sites, historical houses decorated for the holidays, and annual pageants to intrigue and delight the traveler.

In the small towns and villages, school, church, and community groups all take part in the holiday celebration. Even though some New England schools, influenced by Puritan tradition, did not provide for a school Christmas holiday until the early 1880s, the school has been a participant in Christmas activities for many years. Trees decorated by students, classroom displays, window decorations, assignment of Christmas-related history and literature readings, class parties, and musical programs occupy at least part of the children's time in the weeks of December. Ethnic backgrounds and religious observances (in

Ingenuity knows no bounds in an effort to cheer up a sick friend, in the hospital for Christmas.

particular, Hanukkah remembrances as observed by Jewish children) are incorporated into the school holiday program. In church-affiliated schools, nativity pageants and service projects are annual events.

Much preparation also is taking place in the churches. Many congregations hold holiday bazaars at which baked goods and arts and crafts items are offered for sale. Besides raising money for church upkeep, the bazaars offer a showcase for handicrafts unavailable elsewhere: quilts, handloomed weavings, hooked and rag rugs, prosaic dishtowels and aprons enlivened with fancy work, elaborately stitched sachets, and pungent pomanders. Herbs, dried flowers and weeds, and home-canned pickles and relishes are also common finds at New England holiday bazaars.

Church caroling groups loaded with decorations and gifts visit shut-ins and hospitals. With an eye toward the needs of particular individuals, the churches contribute gift packages of food, toys, clothing, or other items. This is done with reserve and respect for pride and privacy typical of the area. Christmas generosity is organized and distributed with caring efficiency.

Several congregations may join together to produce a large pageant or play. "Paradise plays" are occasionally staged during the first weeks of Advent. These relate the story of creation and the fall of man, then the prophets' tales of the coming of a Messiah. Nativity plays, or living manger scenes, are common in the two weeks prior to Christmas.

The children of the congregation are also busy in the weeks before Christmas. Can goods may be collected for distribution to the needy. Special lessons are also taught in Sunday school, which reinforce the essentially religious nature of the holiday. Christmas programs, which combine the younger children in an evening of recitation, pantomime, and singing, are presented for parents, relatives, and church members.

Sunday schools were first established in the early nineteenth century as part of a nondenominational movement to instill religious dogma in the young. The American Sunday School Union was organized in Boston in 1824 to provide lesson materials for use to American Protestant church schools. In the early years of the movement, the Puritan prejudice against Christmas was still strong enough to repress holiday observances. However, by 1859, attitudes had changed sufficiently that the *Sunday School Times,* a publication of the American Sunday School Union, contained accounts of celebrations at various individual churches. The Union was, by 1870, preparing, and sending throughout the country, detailed lesson plans outlining Christmas teachings. Aspects of the nonreligious observance of the holiday, for example, gift exchanges and Christmas trees, were included. For many nineteenth century children, this was a first glimpse of Christmas trees and the Dickensian philosophy of charity and good will. In an interesting reversal of roles, these children returned home to teach their parents what was becoming *the* accepted American way to celebrate Christmas. The effects of this movement on the evolvement of a distinct American Christmas were profound.

This crossing of the religious and nonreligious continues today. The use of decorations in the sanctuaries of many Protestant churches was unacceptable until well into the twentieth century. Congregational and other strict Protestant churches continue to ban decorations as pagan and out-of-place in the celebration of Christ's birth. Other denominations hang evergreen roping (the "hanging of the greens" is a tradition in many Episcopal and Roman Catholic parishes, among some Lutherans as well) and add extra candles or an Advent wreath. Still other churches erect Christmas trees and crèches and decorate with poinsettias.

New England towns with a predominate ethnic heritage usually express that particular tradition in their Christmas celebrations. German, Irish, Scandinavian, Slavic, Italian, Dutch, French, and Portuguese populations reenact the customs of their European ancestors. Early American Christmas is also frequently celebrated in the many restored historical sites. These re-creations are carefully researched and are accurate in detail as well as being an enjoyable activity for both spectators and participants.

The traditional American Christmas is based in the family, and the New England celebration is no exception. Despite a multitude of outside activities for all, the center of Christmas is always the renewal of family bonds and the celebration of peace and good will in the home. Animosities are forgotten, and rifts are mended, at least for the duration of the season.

As Christmas Eve approaches, cars, even sleighs, are packed with brightly wrapped packages, boxes of cookies and candy, pies, and all those special family foods. Relatives from everywhere gather for what may be the only meeting of the year. Children play in the snow with cousins twice removed—or is it second cousins? Inside, grown-ups catch up on family news and get acquainted with new in-laws or the youngest of the next generation. Spirits are mixed and toasts made to the warmth of family ties, the sense of belonging.

As travel-weary visitors crawl into borrowed beds, children snuggled below in well-used trundles, the stillness of the large houses comes to match the snowy hush outside. The peace of the season that comes from being home again has arrived.

In rural Maine, New Hampshire, and Vermont, the horse still knows the way.

CHAPTER FOUR

Deck the Halls

THE CHRISTMAS TREE'S FAMILY TREE IS NEARLY IMPOSSIBLE TO ACCURATELY TRACE. THE custom was brought to America by German immigrants, but the practice is much older than Christianity. Plants and trees that remain green throughout the year have always held "special" qualities for human beings. Archaeological evidence suggests that evergreens were hauled into caves at the winter solstice as part of magical rites to ensure that vegetation would return to an otherwise brown and dead earth.

Decking the halls with boughs of holly may be nearly as old. Certainly the ancient Romans "decked" out their houses, temples, and even themselves for festivals, especially the Saturnalia, celebrated annually between the 17th and 19th of December. The Puritans were correct that many Christmas customs are pagan in origin. The simple truth, of course, is that human beings will celebrate a winter holiday and will decorate for the occasion with "greens."

The evergreen has always been valued for both its symbolic and practical use at winter festivals. Since they remain a vibrant green all year and do not shed their leaves, they are a symbol of eternal life. The evergreens—which include coniferous trees, holly, laurel, mistletoe, and boxwood—are also the only attractive natural decorating material available at a time of year when flowering plants and most trees are dormant.

Holly, since ancient times, has figured prominently in both sacred and pagan legend. The burning bush seen by Moses was probably one of a number of evergreen species and may have been a young holly tree. The prickly leaves and red berries have long been associated with the crown of thorns worn by Christ. The ancient Druids considered holly to be of value in dispelling evil spirits. The two forms of holly, prickly and smooth, were said to represent male and female. In medieval England, whichever type was first brought into the house at Christmas determined whether the man or the woman would dominate the household for the coming year.

Holly is native to the eastern seaboard of the United States, and holly orchards in Rhode Island and Connecticut, as well as in Massachusetts, grow the plant in great quantities for commercial use. Modern horticulture has improved the cultivation and propagation of a plant that was once becoming scarce due to overharvesting by enthusiastic holiday decorators.

Mistletoe, like holly, is a frequently used decoration and a symbol of Christmas throughout Europe and America. Although it was regarded as a sacred plant by the ancient Romans and medieval Druids, mistletoe is never found in modern churches. Aside from adding to decorative greenery, its most common use today is as a catalyst for a holiday kiss.

A Scandinavian legend tells of the goddess of love and beauty, Frigga, who cast a spell over her favorite son, Balder, making him invulnerable to anything that originated from air, fire, water, or earth. A crafty evil spirit, determined to kill Balder, made an arrow from the mistletoe plant (which grows on the bark of trees, not directly in the earth). As a result of an elaborate scheme, Balder was struck by the arrow and severely wounded. The combined efforts of all the gods were required to save the youth's life. His grateful mother then blessed the mistletoe, declaring that it should never again be the cause of any harm and granted a kiss to anyone who passed beneath it.

The legend, and the attendant custom, traveled with Swedish and Norwegian immigrants to the New World. As a result, mistletoe, in sprigs or as part of a "kissing ball," hangs in doorways and halls during the holiday season.

While evergreens are used to symbolize everlasting life and the triumph of life over death, candles and other sources of light are prominent in the traditional Christmas, expressing Christ as the light of the world. A common sight in New England is the house with a candle in every window. The custom originated in Boston, where it was introduced by Irish immigrants.

Decking the halls peaked in Victorian America when every available surface was crowned with a touch of Christmas. (From Chatterbox, 1871)

Prior to the wave of immigration to America, the Irish had suffered religious persecution under Protestant Great Britain. Roman Catholic priests were forbidden to celebrate the Mass and were severely punished if caught. Yet the Irish faithful persevered, especially at Christmas. The lighted candle in the window became a sign to passing priests that midnight Mass could be celebrated in that house. The custom was explained to the authorities as a "light in case Mary and Joseph should need it to find their way" and was, for the most part, officially ignored as a harmless folk custom. In this way, the Irish Catholics kept the practice of their faith alive, and the tradition of the window candle was continued as they settled in New England. Boston's Brahmin class, strictly Protestant and of pure English descent, found the lighted candles enchanting and quickly adopted the custom, without understanding the significance or the irony in their own actions.

In the houses and towns of New England, lighting adds to the feeling of warmth, joy, and peace. Candles adorn dining tables and sideboards. The flames of a fireplace provide comfort and cheer as well as warmth. A child may sit for hours, entranced by a small circle of candles with tiny brass angels whirling above, set into motion by the heat of the flames. Each angel carries a stick or wand, and as it circles, it softly strikes two small bells, producing a series of delicate chimes.

Christmas bells come in a variety of shapes and sizes, from jingle bells on sleighs to the massive bells cast by Paul Revere and other colonial craftsmen for early Massachusetts churches. Bells have been baptized, named, and assigned personalities. They are rung on sidewalks by

Santas asking for contributions to help the needy. They herald the arrival of carolers in much the same way as they were used by town criers in the early days of the Colonies. Groups of bell ringers perform intricate melodies as part of the Christmas worship service. They call the people to worship, and they inspire weary shoppers with hymns and carols pealing out over the pre-Christmas rush on busy streets. Snow-covered bells form part of many door decorations, and tiny red and green bells are found alongside the bows of packages beneath the tree.

The ancestors of the modern ornament-laden fir or spruce are as numerous as they are difficult to accurately trace. Besides the use of evergreens, people brought branches of such flowering trees as cherry and hawthorn inside in the fall and, with care and luck, forced them to bloom for Christmas. The early Paradise plays, depicting the fall of Adam and Eve, required a tree that bore apples. Since real apple trees would obviously not suffice in the winter, the players improvised, hanging apples on evergreens cut for the occasion.

In medieval times, pyramids of brush were formed, or branches were hung from the ceiling. Actual cut trees came into use soon afterward, especially in Germany and northern Europe.

The first Christmas tree in New England (although not the first in America) was decorated in 1832 by Charles Follen, a German living in Boston, for his son. A description of the occasion, written by Harriet Martineau, was published by the American Sunday School Union:

I was present at the introduction into the new country of the spectacle of the German tree. . .We were all engaged in sticking on the last seven dozen of wax tapers, and in filling the gilded egg

Top Left. *Candles shining from every window and outdoor lights reflected on snow add a feeling of warmth and serenity to this Manchester, New Hampshire, home.*

Above. *The magic of Christmas includes the little things around which childhood fantasies are woven — perhaps an angel pointed out as a special "favorite."*

35

shells and gay paper cornucopiae with comfits, lozenges, barley sugar. The tree was the top of a young fir, planted in a tub, which was ornamented with moss. Smart dolls and other whimsies glittered in the evergreen, and there was not a twig which had not something sparkling upon it. . . The ornaments were so well hung that no accident happened, except that one doll's petticoat caught fire. There was a sponge tied to the end of a stick to put out any supernumerary blaze, and no harm ensued. . .I have little doubt that the Christmas tree will become one of the most flourishing exotics of New England.

The exotic custom did indeed flourish in New England, as well as in the rest of the country. Within 25 years, the Christmas tree was officially endorsed by the President, when in 1856 Franklin Pierce, a native of New Hampshire, set up the first tree in the White House.

In New England, a Christmas tree is a fir tree, either balsam or Douglas fir. The Scotch, Jack, and long needle pines and spruce trees sold in other areas of the country are greeted with a pursed lip silence by the hide-bound New Englander.

Ornaments manufactured specifically for a Christmas tree were first imported into this country in about 1870. Made in Dresden, Germany, they were cardboard but intricately layered with gold and silver and shaped into three-dimensional forms. Later German inventions that became popular in the United States were tinsel (1878) and angel hair (early 1880s).

Most of the antique ornaments treasured by today's New England families originated in the small town of Lauscha, Germany. The Lauscha glassblowers' operation was primarily a cottage industry, but they produced up to 95 percent of all of the blown-glass ornaments sold in this country prior to 1940. They first developed a formula that gave their blown glass a particular sheen. A gas flame system was then perfected in the 1860s, so that the workers could have an even, intense heat supply. At the same time, a process for blowing glass into molds was developed, and Lauscha became the center of a rapidly growing ornament industry.

The ornaments produced were detailed, well made, and wonderfully inventive. Family assembly lines, each member with an assigned task, turned out fruits, vegetables, pickles, pine cones, acorns, icicles, musical instruments (some with whistles that actually played), Santas, animals, fish, and the familiar birds with elegant tails of spun glass. Ships of all kinds, with rigging of real silver wire, were marvels of delicacy and, yet, affordable. The Lauscha ornaments were first sold in the U.S. in 1881 by F.W. Woolworth in his variety store at Lancaster, Pennsylvania. By 1890, Woolworth was personally traveling

*Narrow city streets, through which centuries of New
England history have marched, glow with holiday spirit and life.*

Delicate sailboats, with silver rigging, and faded angels, kept aloft in fragile hot-air balloons, were made for American Christmas trees in Lauscha, Germany. Now rare keepsakes, such ornaments were, during the first part of the twentieth century, imported by the hundreds of thousands and sold in dime stores.

to Germany to buy hundreds of thousands of ornaments for his chain of dime stores, the success of which was largely based upon the importation of inexpensive Christmas decorations. Lauscha survived World War I and the Depression, but the division of Germany after World War II left it behind the Iron Curtain, separated from its American market. The Corning Glass Works, prodded in part by a Woolworth executive, began to manufacture glass ornaments in huge quantities, and the quality work of the German artisans largely disappeared.

Martin Luther is credited with being the first to illuminate a Christmas tree. He was inspired by starlight on an evergreen forest and tried to recapture this effect with candles on a small fir tree. Candles, thereafter, became a standard decoration. The soft, warm glow of a candlelit tree first glimpsed through parlor doors was an unforgettable sight; one that few Americans today have ever known. Fire, of course, was the difficulty. While buckets of sand and water were usually kept next to the tree, the danger was still very real. Nineteenth century newspapers are filled with accounts of Christmas fires, of children, dressed in paper angel costumes, dancing too close to the candles. The problem was attacked with characteristic vigor by American inventors. New and purportedly safer candleholders were marketed yearly. Finally, American technology was brought to bear.

The first electric Christmas lights were a one-of-a-kind set, made in 1882. Each tiny bulb was individually blown and wired by Edison workmen for a company executive. The idea immediately became fashionable, but only among the very wealthy; an average tree cost $1,000 to 2,000 to electrify.

In 1890 General Electric bought from Edison the right to manufacture Christmas lights. GE soon came out with the first "practical" set. They were, however, still expensive and required the services of an electrician.

Technology continued to improve, and by the 1920s, the average American family could afford electric lights on their tree. Sets in this period could even be purchased with a battery, for the farm family still without electricity. Progress continued with parallel wiring, a boon to American fathers nagged into searching through a fully decorated tree for the single burned-out bulb causing the entire string to go out. Novelty lights also appeared: bulbs, from Austria and Japan, shaped and painted like Santa, reindeer, snowmen, and even cartoon characters; the bubble lights of the 1950s, which refused to stand up straight; and miniature Italian lights, which nearly doomed the American NOMA® bulb to extinction.

Today in New England, the cheery, standard Christmas light of youthful memory continues to glow through front windows. And even candles are making a comeback. Candleholders, still manufactured in Germany where electric tree lights never caught on, are being imported in ever increasing numbers. Christmas is, unquestionably, a celebration of personal memory and tradition.

Schools and day-care centers enter into the spirit of the season with holiday crafts. Santa's helper is often on hand to provide scissors and glue.

CHAPTER FIVE

'Twas the Night Before

CHRISTMAS EVE. CONFUSION REIGNS OVER LAUGHTER, RINGING DOORBELLS, BARKING dogs, hardy greetings, and youthful whispers. The house is filled with a smell unique to this one night: simmering oysters, evergreen, hickory logs, and eggnog. With conspiratory giggles, gifts too large to hide indoors or bought too late are smuggled into the house. Children's excitement reaches a pitch near hysteria as grandfathers and older brothers tease and grandmothers scold.

And outside. It is miraculously quiet. The snow, falling in unperturbable dignity, fills the night with silence and an eerie reflected light. The air is cold and still. A current of smoke intermittently gives off the reassuring smell of burning fireplace logs.

The rush is over. Merchants have closed their doors, wished one another a merry Christmas, and hurried home to their own celebrations. Traffic is sparse. Way off, there is a jingling of tire chains muffled in packed snow. Across the street colored lights and candles glow from windows and shine briefly from a doorway opened to admit a caller on foot.

All across New England, dinner is being served. On Christmas Eve, it is a simple meal, generally only one dish—stew or thick soup. Oyster stew with Vermont common crackers is a tradition common to many families. Dessert is fruitcake or apple pie with cheddar cheese. Trays of cookies and candy stand on the sideboard, tempting passers-by. The table is soon cleared, as preparations for the Christmas Day feast are the main priority.

The tree stands tall and full in the living room. It may be partially decorated by Christmas Eve, but at least some of the finishing touches are saved for this night. Strings of popcorn and cranberries are draped over the branches. An ornament is moved from place to place, usually by the tallest available child, under the direction of an experienced grandparent. The entire family is present as the youngest child is lifted up high to place the star at the top of the tree. Many New England households adhere to the old tradition of not lighting the tree until Christmas Eve, as a symbol of the light that has come into the world with the birth of Christ.

It is the church, however, that is the focal point of Christmas Eve. The streets and parking lots around the churches begin to fill, and young stars of Christmas plays, clutching their broomstick shepherd's crooks and tinfoil halos, scamper to the doors. Glittering cardboard stars are hoisted in countless sanctuaries, as white-draped juvenile angels announce the Savior's coming. Joseph and Mary make their way to the stable, and amid innocent smiles and giggles, the story unfolds.

Beautiful poinsettias and massive candles enrich Christmas observances in some New England churches and cathedrals.

Some services reflect a modern attitude, with trees and banners in the church, guitars and verse included in the worship. Children may bring gifts wrapped in white to place before the manger scene. Prayers and songs are delivered with exuberance by even the smallest members of the congregation.

Other services are more formal but no less joyful. Episcopal churches draped in greenery hold the traditional service of lessons and carols, where the Christmas gospel and prayers alternate with seasonal hymns. Roman Catholic churches observe the birth of Christ with the celebration of midnight Mass. The service from St. Peter's Basilica in Rome, celebrated by the pope, is broadcast on television worldwide.

Candle ceremonies are traditional in many denominations. Each person attending the service is given a small candle. During the final hymn, flame from a central candle is passed from person to person, and every candle in the church is lighted. The overhead lights are dimmed, and the last verses are sung in the flickering light of the small flames. The final blessing is given before the candles are extinguished and the congregation dismissed.

In many homes, children are then hurried off to bed, urged to at least a semblance of sleep by warnings that Santa Claus does not visit houses whose occupants are still awake. Other families exchange a Christmas Eve gift, with each person permitted to open one, but only one, of the tantalizing presents beneath the tree. Equally traditional, at least for the modern era, is the parent, awake far into the night, surrounded by pieces of dollhouse or bicycle, muttering over the instruction sheet in an attempt to find the elusive bolt 43B. Meanwhile, the stockings are stuffed and Santa's bounty arranged to await the children, who will sneak down the stairs before it is barely dawn.

European custom called for the hanging of small gifts from the branches of the Christmas tree. This has been almost completely replaced in America by gifts beneath the tree and the hanging of Christmas stockings. Originally, the stockings hung were those actually worn by the children. They were attached to the fireplace mantle, as newly washed stockings in everyday life were often hung by the fire to dry.

The connection of stockings to Christmas derives from one of the many St. Nicholas legends. According to the story, a once wealthy man, now impoverished, had three daughters but no money for their support or their dowries. As each girl came of an age to marry, her dowry was secretly supplied by St. Nicholas, who tossed a bag of gold through an open window during the night. On one occasion, the money fell into the girl's stocking, which was hanging near the fire. Modern American children still receive trinkets from Santa Claus in this way, and the customary orange in the toe of the stocking takes its origin from the bag of gold in the legend.

Other items in the stocking have symbolic meaning, although some gifts become "stocking stuffers" merely because they are of the proper size. Nuts symbolize birth and fertility. Coins, sweets, and other items formerly considered to be luxuries are also placed in the stocking at times. The stockings are hung from the mantel not only because of the association with fire and hearth in the legend, but also because Santa Claus is traditionally said to make his entrance down the chimney.

Some of the legendary figures that contributed to the formation of the American Santa could have managed a chimney descent far more readily than the familiar modern plump character with a large sack of toys slung across his back. The evolution of Santa Claus owes much to the European ancestry of our first settlers, but is also indebted to the inventiveness of native-born artists and writers.

The real St. Nicholas was a bishop in Asia Minor during the first half of the fourth century. He was identified with children and with the giving of gifts, particularly to the needy (as the story of the poor man with three daughters illustrates). An incident whereby he saved a storm-tossed ship from destruction also led to his being considered the patron of sailors, an element that was not lost in early maritime New England.

Nicholas, as bishop, would visit the people under his care and see to their spiritual instruction and welfare as well as their material needs. Therefore, it became the custom throughout Europe for individuals to dress in mock bishop's robes and visit local children on the eve of December 6, St. Nicholas' Day. The saint-character would question the children about their behavior and hear them recite the Catechism, rewarding good children with gifts. He was accompanied by a goblin or creature (who sometimes entered the house through the chimney), representing the alternative to a reward for good behavior. Gradually, the spiritual elements became less important; the emphasis shifted toward gifts, merriment, mischief, and other remnants of pagan festivals. The bishop's costume persisted, however, and is still used in some European countries today.

The leaders of the Protestant Reformation violently opposed the character of St. Nicholas, as well as the offshoots found in the British Father Christmas and the Scandinavian yuletide elves. The celebration, the Reformers maintained, was of the birth of the Christ Child, and gifts, if they were to appear, should come from God. The concept is still quite strong in Germany, where children write letters to the Christ Child early in Advent, asking for their Christmas wishes in the same way that American children send lists to Santa Claus.

The Christ Child (*Kristkindl* in German), the elves, the gift-giving

Leaving a treat for Santa is a tradition that spans hundreds of years. Pre-Christian people of Ireland left food out for house spirits during the winter solstice.

bishop, and similar legends, all came to the American colonies. Puritan repression of Christmas was strong, however, and anti-British sentiment encouraged adoption of customs from lands other than England. The German *Kristkindl* dropped all resemblance to the infant Jesus and became Kriss Kringle, assuming at the same time some of the characteristics of the elves and dwarfs popular with Swedish and Danish immigrants.

The Dutch in New York held fast to St. Nicholas. Despite religious repression, interest in the holiday revived, and an Americanized St. Nick (or *Sinter Klaas* in Dutch) appeared. Gradually the date of his visits was moved to coincide with the increasingly popular December 25 holiday instead of the traditional December 5. He was said to ride in a

Santa Claus became "Santa Claus"—fat, bearded, suited in red, hoisting a bag of toys—with the help of Thomas Nast, a nineteenth century illustrator for Harper's Weekly.

wagon filled with gifts, which could fly at rooftop height. Washington Irving was among the first of the popular writers to characterize this new St. Nicholas in his 1809 *History of New York*.

In 1822, Clement Moore, a New York theologian and onetime resident of Newport, Rhode Island, wrote his now famous poem "A Visit from St. Nicholas" (popularly known as "The Night Before Christmas"). Moore was slow to claim authorship of the classic, and some still question whether or not he actually was responsible for the poem. Nevertheless, it forever changed the image of St. Nicholas from lean bishop to plump, jolly, red-cheeked, bearded little man. Moore also introduced the popular sleigh and reindeer, more suitable transportation than a wagon for the climate of the Northeast. This source and Irving's work formed the basis for the first illustrations to depict Santa Claus in his modern form.

Illustrator Thomas Nast, the creator of such famous symbols as the Republican elephant and the Democratic donkey, painted a series of Santa Claus illustrations for *Harper's Weekly* magazine's Christmas issues. These were printed from 1863 through 1886 and established the image of Santa firmly in the minds of Americans. Nast was also responsible for Santa's North Pole address and for the concept of his workshop, where toys and gifts were manufactured.

Later artists, writers, and advertising agencies added the finishing details. Mrs. Santa Claus first appeared in an 1889 children's story. The Coca-Cola Company, beginning in 1931, marketed the red-suited St. Nick worldwide, as a spokesman for its products. In 1939, a red-nosed reindeer was invented as a promotional handout by Montgomery Ward and Company. The store later sold the copyright for the animal back to its original author, ad agency copywriter Robert May, who mentioned the idea to his brother-in-law, songwriter Johnny Marks. He composed a song for Gene Autry that was an instant success. The 1949 song assured Rudolph the red-nosed reindeer his promised place in history.

Theologians and church officials have condemned Santa Claus. In many ways, however, the popularized saint has protected the religious symbols of the holiday from commercial corruption. Santa Claus has been embraced by a nation with a Puritan heritage, in part so that Christ would *not* appear on billboards and in department stores. St. Nick, the symbol of good cheer and good will, can sell presents as well as give them, stand on a street corner and solicit donations for the poor, and provide a lap and an ear for children and their wishes. He can live in harmony with the sacred celebration of Christ's birth, simply providing an additional element to the season. This is especially true in New England. Here various traditions melt into one unique set of customs, and the spirit of Christmas overcomes the major confrontations between the religious traditions and the secular ones.

New England family Christmases begin early in the morning, even

earlier than is usual for the New Hampshire or Vermont native. Excited
children exclaim over every present (with the possible exception of
the new shirt and tie from the more practical side of the family).
Wrappings are piled into the fireplace, bright colors wilting in the flame.
Grandmothers may save choice bits for next year, and a wayward
ribbon usually ends up around the neck of the family dog.

While the kitchen is crowded with people and the makings for the
feast, others are outdoors, shoveling a path to the road or making
angels in the snow. The family may attend an early church service or
spend the morning in conversation, games, or trying out the new sled or
skates.

Christmas dinner is invariably a midafternoon meal, but it is worth
the long, hungry wait. The table is pulled out, all the leaves added,
and the best linen tablecloth spread. Candlesticks are ringed with holly
and pine cones; greens are everywhere. Card tables are set up to
accommodate the overflow, usually the children. Platters and bowls are
brought in, everything in great quantity. As the family is assembled,
hands are joined and the head of the household asks the blessing on the
bounty before them.

The traditional Thanksgiving feast of the Puritans has found its
place at the Christmas season now. Most families enjoy a large bird,
usually turkey but often goose or capon. It is stuffed with a moist bread

stuffing, complemented in New England by oysters and chestnuts. The side dishes are rich with cream sauces, especially the vegetables—onions or peas. More seafood dishes, scalloped oysters, for example, may be evident in this region where seafood is plentiful. Pickles, "put up" in the fall from the last of the summer garden, are brought from the cellar and arranged with carrots and celery on a relish plate. Cranberries, in sauces, rings, and salads, add tart contrast to the rich meal.

Amid claims that no one could possibly eat another bite, dessert is served. Suet or plum pudding, which never did contain plums, is an English tradition. This dish is sometimes served with a flaming brandy sauce, other times with hard sauce, called "hard" because it may contain hard liquor. Various types of pies are also present, including the familiar mince pie, once the object of much controversy.

Mincemeat originated in the Middle Ages and was originally a mixture of pork, venison, game bird, rabbit, suet, fruits, molasses, and spices. The fragrant, spicy combination was used to symbolize the gifts of the Magi, and the mincemeat was baked in a deep rectangular pastry shell, resembling a manger. A clay or pastry figure of the Christ Child was placed on the top of the pie. New England Puritans considered this

Christmas morning spans all generations and all generation gaps.

custom sacrilegious and outlawed it. In its place, colonial women substituted a round pie garnished with holly sprigs. The meat ingredients are often omitted from modern mincemeat, although traditional recipes still contain beef and suet. It is said that Little Jack Horner's "Christmas pie" was a mince pie, although mincemeat, like plum pudding, had no plums in it for the boy to pull out with his thumb. The rhyme refers to a man named Thomas Horner, a messenger from a church official to the court of King Henry VIII. In an effort to appease the land-greedy king, this churchman had baked a mince pie that also contained the deeds to several valuable pieces of property. He commanded Horner to take it to the king as a Christmas present. (In this way it was hoped that Henry could be prevented from appropriating more church property.) Horner, aware of the special contents of the pie, filched one of the deeds—a "plum" of sorts—for himself and thus became a wealthy landowner. The memory of his crime has been lost, but the children's nursery rhyme it inspired remains.

After the meal is finished and the table cleared, the family, too full for active sports or games, might join in singing Christmas carols. Someone plays the piano or, if none of the family has that talent, turns on a recording of Christmas songs. Music is inseparable from Christmas. Even those who believe themselves to be totally nonmusical will hum or sing a few notes from the familiar carols.

Many Christmas songs originated in or near New England. Henry Wadsworth Longfellow was born in Portland, Maine, although he is usually associated with Massachusetts. His Christmas hymn, "I Heard the Bells on Christmas Day," was written in 1863, at the height of the Civil War, shortly after the battle of Gettysburg. Longfellow's son had been wounded in that battle, and he shared in a national feeling of grief and hopelessness brought on by the tragedy of the war. But the message conveyed by the Christmas bells—the repetition, as in the refrain, "of peace on earth, good-will to men"—was one of eternal hope, of the eventual triumph of peace over war, of good over evil.

Another carol piece in the midst of strife was written prior to the outbreak of the Civil War. In 1849, the pastor of the Unitarian Church at Wayland, Massachusetts, Edmund H. Sears, urged the world to abandon thoughts of war, rest from toil, and "hear the angels sing." His "It Came Upon a Midnight Clear" was originally published as a poem in the Bostonian *Christian Register*. It was used as such in Christmas programs before being set to music the following year by Richard Willis, also of Boston. Although the lyrics do not specifically mention Christmas, the theme of the season predominates.

Seven years later, John Henry Hopkins, then Rector of Christ Church, Williamsport, Pennsylvania, wrote both words and music of "We Three Kings of Orient Are." This carol describes the journey of the three kings from the East to the site of Christ's birth. Each verse is assigned to a different king, which makes the carol a popular one for use in Christmas or Epiphany plays. It was published in Hopkins's later collection, *Carols, Hymns, and Songs.* This book was a major resource for and influence on the renewed interest in carols and group singing that took place in New England during the Victorian era.

Phillips Brooks, a prominent Episcopal clergyman, was a renowned preacher of the nineteenth century and eventually became the Bishop of Massachusetts. He spent a year traveling through the Holy Land and in 1865 attended Christmas Eve services in Bethlehem. The experience later inspired the words to "O Little Town of Bethlehem," which he wrote in 1868 for his parish Sunday school to perform. The music to accompany Brooks's words was written by Lewis Redner, organist of Holy Trinity Church in Philadelphia. Redner received the idea for the melody in a dream, and the song as we now know it was performed by the children that Christmas.

Not all Christmas music, at that time or now, has a sacred theme. Popular tunes, secular songs, and traditional ballads from America's European heritage also make up a part of the Christmas repertoire. "Deck the Halls" is a Welsh carol, celebrating the decorating of homes,

*The table cleared, the dishes washed, aunts, uncles, and
cousins join in the singing of carols.*

feasting merrymaking, and song. The exact date of its composition
cannot be determined, but the pattern of a stanza of lyrics followed by a
line of single syllables (fa-la-la) is typical of the madrigals of the Middle
Ages. Many of the pagan customs that thrived at that time, from the
Yule log to mummers' festivals, are mentioned. The carol was also once
employed by Mozart in a classical composition. "Deck the Halls"
celebrates both the mystery of the Christian celebration and the carefree
abandon of the pagan feast. This combination is typical of the
American Christmas observance.

The one element most readily identified with the New England
holiday (and indeed with the nostalgic American Christmas ideal) is
snow. Natives of warmer climates are pitied at this time of year, and
vacationing or transplanted Northerners who spend Christmas in the
South came to feel that they are missing an essential part of the season.
New England snows are heralded in song: "Let It Snow," "The Christmas
Song," "White Christmas," and, of course, "Jingle Bells."

"Jingle Bells," in fact, says nothing about Christmas, has a second
verse that contains poor sentiment and even worse syntax, but remains
immensely popular. Christmas and the one-horse open sleigh, once a
standard and necessary pairing in New England, remain rooted in the
nation's holiday lore. The song was written by James Pierpont (uncle of
the notoriously wealthy native of Hartford, Connecticut, J. Pierpont
Morgan), who himself was later to move to the South, probably never
to experience snow again.

The New England climate is also a favorite setting for Christmas
television specials and holiday movies, which may be the twentieth
century's greatest contribution to American Christmas lore. The
seasonal presentation of plays with a Christmas theme is a very old
custom. Paradise and nativity plays, as well as fanciful masques, were

51

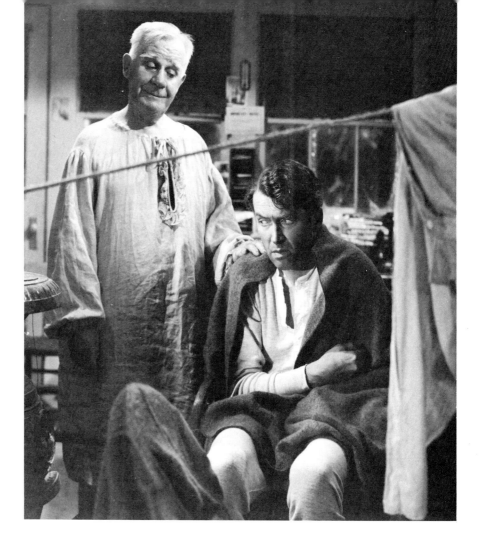

James Stewart and Henry Travers in It's A Wonderful Life. *Hollywood's version of Christmas in New England has become part of the national lore with annual broadcasts of classic, holiday films.*

staged throughout the Middle Ages. Dickens' carol stories were dramatized soon after they were written. Operas and ballets, for example, Tchaikovsky's *Nutcracker*, have been presented annually for well over a century. But the American Christmas drama differs in its light-hearted approach and vast appeal. Hollywood, throughout the 1930s and especially during World War II, turned out for Christmas audiences movies that fused all the various American myths and customs into a vision of the "ideal" Christmas. While popular when first released, the films achieved their classic appeal with the advent, in the 1950s, of television. Shown annually by television stations across the nation, these films, with their gentle and often whimsical messages, have been integrated into the family celebration of the holiday.

The use of New England as the setting for these films is very much a part of their appeal: this is what Christmas should, and perhaps can, be like. The Connecticut inn at the holiday season was immortalized by Bing Crosby and Fred Astaire in the 1942 movie "Holiday Inn." The most memorable part of the film (indeed the "title song" to many viewers) is Irving Berlin's "White Christmas." Between its release and 1970, over 135 million copies of the recording were sold around the world.

Another movie similar in spirit is "Christmas in Connecticut," which shows Hollywood's concept of a New England farm at Christmas. The portrayal is not completely accurate, but the scenes have established themselves in the imaginations of the American moviegoer as representing what the typical Christmas in New England should be.

Although the Christmas movie seldom centers on the story of the Nativity, angels and other heavenly creatures appear regularly. Cary Grant played a problem-solving angel in "The Bishop's Wife," which dealt with the personal and professional woes of a New England bishop. The angel eventually brings about miraculous solutions, just in time for Christmas, and all is well for the bishop and his wife. The spirit of generosity, happiness, and freedom from care at Christmas was especially prominent in films made during and immediately following World War II.

The best of the Christmas classics is probably "It's a Wonderful Life," which features another kindhearted, if bumbling, angel. In the movie, James Stewart plays a self-sacrificing banker in a small New England town. He helps so many people, at the cost of his own advancement and security, that he feels trapped and hopeless; all sense of self-worth is lost. But with the angel's assistance, Stewart is able to see his own contribution and how each man's life touches a multitude of others.

"It's a Wonderful Life" not only depicts life in a small New England town, but it also examines the values central to Christmas. Made by the talented Frank Capra, the film reconfirms the spiritual value of family and friends, as well as the American notion of freedom and personal dignity. Capra, self-effacingly, refers to his work in films as "Capra-corn," but "It's a Wonderful Life" and "Meet John Doe," another Capra movie shown during the holiday season, offer a vision of hope and peace that pulls them above their contrived stories. Like Dickens' picture of Christmas in Victorian England, Capra's reflection of twentieth century America continues to touch and reach new audiences.

Sunday school classes trim a classroom tree, then exchange cards or small gifts. Later, the cards are used to decorate the walls.

The Burning of the Greens—the tradition, which continues in some areas of New England, began in ancient Rome as a ceremony to ward off evil spirits.

Christmas Day draws to a close. Everyone is tired, but it is a good tiredness after a full and satisfying day. The children fall asleep clutching new toys, waiting for the morning so they can play again. School vacation lasts until the beginning of January, and there is time for an extended family visit.

The day after Christmas, for the typical American adult, may be one of the best days of the year. The staging of a traditional Christmas celebration, from addressing cards in early December to washing dishes after Christmas dinner, consumes incredible amounts of time and effort. The day after is a day of rest. The kitchen is full of leftovers, generally nibbled on throughout the day; everyone simply helps himself. The adults can enjoy the kids at play, company still in residence, friends paying calls, or the idea that nothing more *must* be done, at least for this one day.

For the whole family, the days after Christmas may be filled with recreation. Ski slopes and frozen ponds are full; both residents and tourists are eager to enjoy the winter fun. In prime ski areas, such as Stowe, Vermont, the attraction of the snow-covered mountainside is an important industry. Country inns and lodges, when the weather cooperates, are filled to capacity. They offer after-ski activities and

*Church drama productions continue throughout the season. A favorite
selection is the Shakespeare comedy,* Twelfth Night.

School is dismissed for the holidays, and the entire family heads for the ski slopes. Winter sports are learned at an early age in a climate where snow predominates from November to March.

refreshments in addition to lodging. Hot buttered rum or mulled wine, sipped in front of a roaring fire, is a favorite of the chilled and weary skier.

The twelve days of Christmas counted off in the popular song span the time between Christmas and Epiphany, or Twelfth Night (January 6). Epiphany (meaning "manifestation") is regarded as that day when the Magi arrived at the scene of the Nativity. It also traditionally marks the end of the Christmas season. On that day, decorations are taken down in homes and churches. According to pagan legend, the greenery must be burned, in order to drive away evil spirits. Other ornaments are packed away carefully, to recreate their magic the following year.

New Year's Eve in New England, as in all of America, is a time for still another celebration. On this occasion, the merriment, of course, centers

New Year's Eve celebration in Boston retains the flavor of old time mumming. Costumes, banners, and balloons add to the raucous merriment.

on the adults. The traditional party to usher out the old year and welcome in the new dates back to the Roman feast of Kalends (from which the word "calendar" is also derived). Modern festivities often resemble the Roman bacchanalia. The hour of midnight is announced with the singing of "Auld Lang Syne," blowing of noisemakers, and much exchanging of good wishes for a happy and prosperous new year.

Until fairly recent times, New Year's Day was a highly social occasion. Houses were thrown open to all who cared to pay a call, hense the term "open-house." For people of English descent, it was considered very good luck if the first visitor of the new year was a young man of fair features. Arrangements were often made to ensure that this first visitor fit the bill, especially if a daughter of marriageable age planned to be "at home."

At the White House in Washington, open-house meant exactly that: the President stood throughout the day shaking hands with whomever, no matter how high or low, walked in off the street. This custom did not end until Herbert Hoover's administration during the Depression.

In New England, tradition holds more weight than televised football, and the open-house on New Year's Day continues, although perhaps as the exception, rather than the rule. Calls are made and greetings of the day extended in a ceremony that officially brings to a close one season and inaugurates the next.

CHAPTER SIX

IT'S CHRISTMASTIME IN THE CITY

BOSTON AT ANY TIME OF THE YEAR IS A BUSY METROPOLITAN CENTER, A CULTURAL monument, an attraction for tourists, and home to an unending variety of people. Boston at Christmas is an urban wonderland. Thousands of lights sparkle on decorations of immense scale. Shoppers crowd into every store, as intent on the spectacle as on their purchases.

One of the major attractions is Boston Common. Since 1921, the massive and splendidly decorated community Christmas tree has occupied a place of honor. Skaters glide across the Public Garden pond, looking like a nostalgic Christmas card come to life. The Nativity scene takes place in a full-sized stable and uses live volunteer "actors." Santa is in residence, of course — in fact, the City Council of 1949 even petitioned the mayor of Boston that the Santa on the Common be the only Santa Claus permitted in the city!

Department store displays evoke awe and wonder in the most hard-hearted adult. Children stand enchanted in front of the animated life-sized winter scenes and fantasy characters at Jordan Marsh. Windows at Filene's depict Christmas in colonial times with meticulous detail.

The open-air market is a throng of activity. Everyone generally ignores the winter weather as gift-seekers wedge themselves three-deep in front of carts and booths. Young children and an occasional dog dart under and around package-laden grown-ups. Christmas carols from loudspeakers compete with the crowd noises and the vendors in cheery chaos.

On a more subdued level are the museum exhibits, including the annual poinsettia display at Fenway Court. The poinsettia, a traditional symbol of Christmas, is native to Mexico. One of the first American diplomatic ministers to Mexico, Dr. Joel Roberts Poinsett, is credited with introducing the species that now bears his name to this country. The brilliant red or greenish white upper leaves (often mistakenly called flowers) were rapidly accepted here and blended well with the traditional red and green Christmas decorations.

Nights in Boston, especially as Christmas Eve approaches, are filled with pageantry and song. In addition to attending formal concerts, many Bostonians participate in the community carol singing and celebration at the Prudential Center. On Beacon Hill, the nation's oldest organized caroling group gathers every year. The group was founded in 1908 as the Chestnut Street Christmas Organization. Although the membership level has fluctuated over the years, the tradition continues unbroken. The carolers walk up and down the sloping streets, bringing their message of peace on earth, good will toward men, as the city joins in joyful anticipation.

Above. *Boston's Public Garden duck pond is frozen hard in time for Christmas vacation skaters and hockey games.*

Right. *Modern-day Bostonians carry on the tradition of Christmas Eve caroling on Beacon Hill. For over three quarters of a century, musicians and singers have assembled yearly to spread the spirit of Christmas to neighborhood residents.*

Above. *In Roxbury, Massachusetts, the Black Nativity Chorus performs at a candlelight service. Below. The Massachusetts State House, erected in 1798, serves as a backdrop for a living reenactment of the Nativity portrayed on Boston Common.*

Right. *The streets of the city are a crush of shoppers. Fruit stands and kiosks filled with Christmas trinkets lend a European atmosphere and indicate the variety of ethnic backgrounds found in Boston.*

Below. *For generations, sightseers and residents have stopped to marvel at the holiday displays in Filene's windows.*

Above. *John Williams, music director of the Boston Pops, conducts (with a little help from Santa and his toyland friends) a community Christmas sing-along at Boston's Prudential Center.*

Left. *At Christmas, the Gardner Museum's Venetian palm court is the center of a lavish poinsettia display. Built as a house by Isabel Stuart Gardner, a colorful patron of the arts, Fenway Court was, upon her death, permanently opened to the public.*

RECIPES

THE GROANING BOARD

Suet Pudding Sauces

Hot Butter Vanilla Sauce
2 cups sugar
¼ cup cornstarch
pinch of salt
4 cups boiling water
½ cup butter
4 tsp. vanilla
2 tsp. nutmeg (or more, to taste)

(1) Combine sugar and cornstarch in heavy saucepan, making sure to smooth all lumps from cornstarch. (2) Add salt and boiling water. Cook until thick and clear. (3) Continue cooking over low heat for 20 minutes. (4) Beat in butter, vanilla, and nutmeg. (5) Serve hot over pudding.

Hard Sauce
⅔ cup butter.
2 cups confectioners' sugar
2 tsp. vanilla

(1) Cream butter until very soft. (2) Stir in sugar and vanilla. (3) Store in cool place until ready to serve. Rum, sherry, or brandy may be added, if desired. Cream or milk may be added, with additional sugar, to make more sauce.

Mincemeat

1 lb. lean beef, neck meat
2 lbs. tart apples (Jonathan)
1 lb. dried currants
1 lb. seedless raisins
½ lb. suet
1 cup cider
½ tsp. salt
½ tsp. cloves
1 tsp. cinnamon
1 tsp. nutmeg
½ tsp. pepper
¼ lb. of citron, chopped
grated peel & juice of 1 lemon
grated peel & juice of 1 orange
2½ cups sugar
¾ to 1 cup peach pickle juice *or*
    crab apple or pear pickle juice *or*
    ¾ to 1 cup whiskey

(1) Cover meat with water and simmer for 3 hours. Allow to cool. Retain the broth. (2) Wash, peel, and core apples. Wash currants and raisins. Cover apples, currants, and raisins with cold water and soak for 30 minutes. Drain. (3) Put meat, apples, currants, raisins, and suet through a meat grinder. (4) Add to the ground mixture all other ingredients, including part of the beef broth, and simmer for an hour or more. The mincemeat may be canned or frozen. Yield: 2 quarts

Gingerbread Men

2½ cups sifted flour
½ tsp. salt
2 tsp. ginger
½ cup butter
½ cup sugar
½ cup molasses
½ tsp. baking soda
¼ cup hot water

decorations:
red-hots
raisins, seedless

icing:
1 cup sifted confectioners' sugar
¼ tsp. salt
½ tsp. vanilla
1 tbsp. cream

(1) Sift together flour, salt, and ginger; set aside. (2) Melt butter in a large saucepan over low heat. Remove saucepan from heat and mix in sugar and molasses. (3) Dissolve soda in hot water. (4) Add the dry ingredients to the molasses mixture alternately with the soda-water. Begin and end with the dry ingredients. (5) Chill the dough for 2 to 3 hours. (6) Preheat oven to 350°. (7) A little at a time, roll out the dough on a floured pastry cloth to a thickness of ⅛ inch. (8) Cut with gingerbread man cookie cutter and, handling the dough carefully, transfer the cookies to an ungreased cookie sheet. Using red-hots for buttons and raisins for eyes, decorate the gingerbread men. (9) Bake the cookies at 350° for 10 to 12 minutes. (10) Allow cookies to cool for 2 to 3 minutes, then transfer gingerbread men from the sheets to cooling racks. (11) While the cookies cool, prepare the icing. Mix together sugar, salt, and vanilla. Add cream a drop at a time until the icing is smooth and able to hold its shape. (12) Using a decorating tube, trim the gingerbread men with the icing, outlining collars, lapels, cuffs, belts, and boots. (13) After the frosting has set, store the gingerbread men in an airtight container. Yield: 2 dozen

English Toffee

1 lb. butter
2 cups sugar
6 tbsp. water
2 tsp. vanilla
8 oz. sweet chocolate bar
English walnuts, finely chopped

(1) Combine butter, sugar, and water in a large, heavy saucepan over high heat. Stir constantly with a wooden spoon until a candy thermometer registers 290°. (2) Remove pan from heat and quickly stir in vanilla. (3) Pour immediately into a buttered 11 × 17 inch jelly roll pan (cookie sheet with sides). (4) Allow mixture to set slightly. (5) Melt chocolate to the consistency of frosting. (6) As if frosting a cake, spread the chocolate evenly across the candy. Sprinkle the top with finely chopped nuts. (7) Cover with waxed paper and set in a naturally cool place, e.g. an unheated room or protected porch (candy will not set properly in the refrigerator). (8) After the toffee is well set, break into shards with a knife and store in tins. The toffee will last without refrigeration for several months. Yield: 2 lbs.

Bon Bon Cookies

½ cup soft butter
¾ cup sifted confectioners' sugar
1 tbsp. vanilla
1½ cups sifted flour
⅛ tsp. of salt
food coloring

fillings:
nutmeats
chocolate chips, semi-sweet
maraschino cherries, halved

icing:
1 cup sifted confectioners' sugar
1 tbsp. cream
1 tsp. vanilla

(1) Mix thoroughly the butter, sugar, and vanilla. Add food coloring if desired.   (2) Mix in the flour and salt by hand. If, at this point, the dough is too dry to easily handle, add 1 to 2 tablespoons cream.   (3) Wrap approximately a tablespoon of dough around one of the fillings and roll into a ball.   (4) Place the bon bons on an ungreased cookie sheet and bake at 350° for 12 to 15 minutes. (5) Mix together the icing ingredients, adding food coloring if desired.   (6) While the bon bons are still hot, dip them in icing. The tops may be decorated with colored sugar or candy sprinkles. Yield: 2 to 3 dozen cookies.

Cookie Cutter Cookies
(Rolled Sugar Cookies)

1½ cups powdered sugar
1 cup butter, softened
1 egg
1 tsp. vanilla extract
½ tsp. almond extract
2½ cups all-purpose flour
1 tsp. baking soda
1 tsp. cream of tartar

(1) Combine sugar, butter, egg, and extracts.   (2) Cream in remaining ingredients.   (3) Cover and refrigerate 3 or more hours.
(4) Preheat oven to 375°.
(5) Divide dough in halves. Keep the unused half in the refrigerator until needed.   (6) Roll dough out on a floured pastry cloth to a thickness of about ³/₁₆ inch. Cut out cookies with cutters.   (7) Bake on ungreased cookie sheet for 7 to 8 minutes. Cool. Frost and decorate. Yield: 4 to 5 dozen cookies.

Divinity

2 cups granulated sugar
½ cup light corn syrup
½ cup water
2 egg whites
1 tsp. vanilla
½ tsp. almond extract

(1) Stir sugar, corn syrup, and water together over low heat until the sugar is dissolved. Bring mixture to a boil; cover. Boil without stirring until it registers 250° on a candy thermometer (or until a spoonful dropped into cold water forms stiff strands like spun glass).   (2) Beat egg whites until they are stiff.
(3) Pour hot syrup over egg whites and beat until the mixture begins to lose its glossiness.   (4) Add vanilla and almond extract.   (5) Drop by teaspoonfuls onto sheets of waxed paper to cool.

Oyster Stew

2 pints cleaned oysters
½ cup butter
1½ quarts milk
1 pint half-and-half
salt
pepper
paprika

(1) Combine oysters, oyster liquor, butter, and seasonings (to taste) in a saucepan and simmer gently until the oysters begin to curl at the edges. (2) At the same time, heat milk and half-and-half, being careful to avoid scorching. (3) Add oysters to milk and simmer over low heat for up to 2 hours. Yield: 8 to 10 servings

Watermelon Rind Pickles

4 quarts prepared watermelon rind
1 cup salt
2 quarts cold water
2 tbsp. whole cloves
3 sticks cinnamon
2 pieces ginger root
1 lemon, thinly sliced
8 cups sugar
1 quart white vinegar
1 quart water

(1) Trim dark skin and pink flesh from a thick watermelon rind. Cut remaining rind into 1 inch pieces or cubes. (2) Dissolve salt in 2 quarts cold water. (3) Pour salt water over the rind and let stand for 6 hours. Add more cold water, if necessary, to completely cover the rind.

(4) Drain off the salt water. (5) Rinse rind with fresh water and again cover completely with fresh, cold water. (6) Cook rind until just tender. (7) Drain. (8) Tie spices together in a cheesecloth bag. (9) Combine sugar, vinegar, lemon, 1 quart of water, and spice bag and simmer for 10 minutes. (10) Add watermelon rind to mixture and simmer until the rind is clear. If syrup becomes too thick before rind is clear, add additional boiling water. (11) Remove spice bag. (12) Pack, boiling hot, into hot canning jars, leaving ¼ inch head space. (13) Adjust caps. (14) Process for 10 minutes (see processing instructions below). Yield: 7 pints

Processing Instructions

The hot water-bath method is used to process preserves, rhubarb, tomatoes, and pickles. To process food by the hot water-bath method, put water in the canner* and heat it on a stove. Containers of cold-packed food may be placed in the canner when the water is warm or cold. Put hot-packed food in when the water is hot. The water *must* completely cover the tops of the jars or cans. Start to time the processing when the water begins to boil gently. The time required for processing varies among foods and also often depends on the size of the container.

After being processed, containers of food are removed from the canner and are cooled. Jars of food are cooled by letting them stand at room temperature. Place them a few inches apart on a wood or plastic surface or on a surface covered with cloth towels or paper towels. Do not cool the jars on a glass, metal, or tile surface.

*A water-bath canner is a metal container deep enough so that jars or cans are completely covered with water during processing. Any deep metal container may be used. Some water-bath canners have close-fitting lids to enable the water to heat rapidly. A water-bath canner has a metal or wooden rack to keep the jars from touching the hot bottom of the canner. Several layers of clean cloth also may serve as a rack.

Crab Apple Pickles

2 quarts Whitney crab apples, with stems
1½ tbsp. whole cloves
1½ tbsp. whole allspice
2 sticks cinnamon
6 cups sugar
3 cups vinegar
3 cups water

(1) Run a large needle through each crab apple to prevent bursting. (2) Combine spices and tie these together in a cheesecloth bag. (3) Combine sugar, vinegar, water, and bag of spices in a large sauce pan and boil for 5 minutes. (4) Place a layer of crab apples in the pan of boiling syrup and cook gently until the apples are nearly tender.

Carefully remove apples from syrup and repeat procedure until all apples are cooked. (5) Place the cooked crab apples in a large pot and pour boiling syrup over apples. (6) Cover and let stand in a cool place for 12 to 18 hours. (7) Drain syrup from crab apples. (8) Carefully pack the crab apples in hot canning jars, leaving ¼ inch head space. (9) Remove the spice bag from the syrup and bring the mixture to a boil. (10) Pour boiling syrup over the apples, leaving ¼ inch head space. (11) Adjust the caps. (12) Process pints and quarts in boiling water bath for 15 minutes (see processing instructions below). Yield: 6 pints

Bread and Butter Pickles

1 quart cucumbers
1 large onion
1 cup vinegar
1 cup water
1 tsp. mustard seed
1 tsp. celery seed
½ tsp. turmeric
1 cup sugar

(1) Slice unpeeled cucumbers until you have a full quart. (2) Slice onion. (3) Soak cucumbers and onion in salt water for 4 hours. Drain. (4) Add vinegar, water, mustard seed, celery seed, turmeric, and sugar to cucumbers and onion; boil for 5 minutes or until the cucumbers are tender. (5) Pack in canning jars and seal airtight. (6) Process for 5 minutes in boiling water bath (see processing instructions below). (7) Cool jars of pickles at room temperature. Yield: 2 pints

Wait until glass jars of food have cooled at least 12 hours and then check the seals. To test metal lids that have a sealing compound, first remove the screw bands. If a metal lid bends slightly inward, the jar is probably sealed correctly. To be sure, carefully lift the jar by holding the edges of the lid with the fingers of one hand. Keep your other hand under the jar in case it falls. If your fingers can support the weight of the jar, it is properly sealed. Glass jars sealed with such lids may be stored with or without the screw bands.

To test a jar sealed with a porcelain-lined zinc cap and a rubber ring, turn the jar over in your hands. If liquid leaks from the lid, the jar has not been properly sealed.

Even if jars are checked for proper sealing on the day after processing, a faulty seal might not be seen. About a week after processing, check for liquid leaking from the seam or lid. The seals of all jars and cans should be checked occasionally during storage. Be sure to label the containers and store them properly. Before using any canned food, check it for spoilage.

Deck the Hall with Boughs of Holly

Old Welsh Carol

Allegro

1. Deck the hall with boughs of hol-ly,
2. See the blaz-ing Yule be-fore us,
3. Fast a-way the old year pass-es,

Fa la la la la, la la la la,

'Tis the sea-son to be jol-ly,
Strike the harp and join the cho-rus,
Hail the new, ye lads and lass-es,

Fa la la la la, la la la la.

Don we now our gay ap-par-rel,
Fol-low me in mer-ry meas-ure,
Sing we joy-ous all to-geth-er,

Fa_la la_la la la la,

Troll the an-cient Yule-tide car-ol,
While I tell of Yule-tide treas-ure,
Heed-less of the wind and weath-er,

Fa la la la la la la la.

From *The International Book of Christmas Carols,*
by Walter Ehret & George K. Evans. ©1980.
Reprinted by permission of The Stephen Greene Press, Brattleboro, Vermont.

Jingle Bells

Dashing through the snow
In a one-horse open sleigh,
O'er the fields we go
Laughing all the way;

Bells on bob-tail ring,
Making spirits bright;
O what fun it is to sing
A sleighing song tonight!

James Pierpont [WE]

It Came Upon the Midnight Clear

Richard S. Willis, 1850

CRAFTS

ALL THE TRIMMINGS

Popcorn and Cranberry Garland

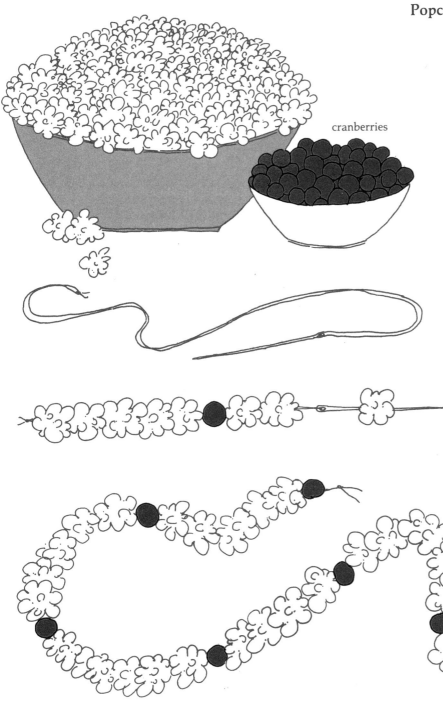

cranberries

Materials:

- popcorn
- cranberries
- needle
- heavy thread

1—Thread a medium-sized needle with 72 inches of heavy thread. Double back and knot the end.
2—Pass the needle through the center of five pieces of popcorn and then through one cranberry.
3—Repeat this pattern (or a variation of your own) until the string is full.

4—Remove the needle and knot the end of the thread.
5—The completed garlands may be tied together at the ends to form one long garland.

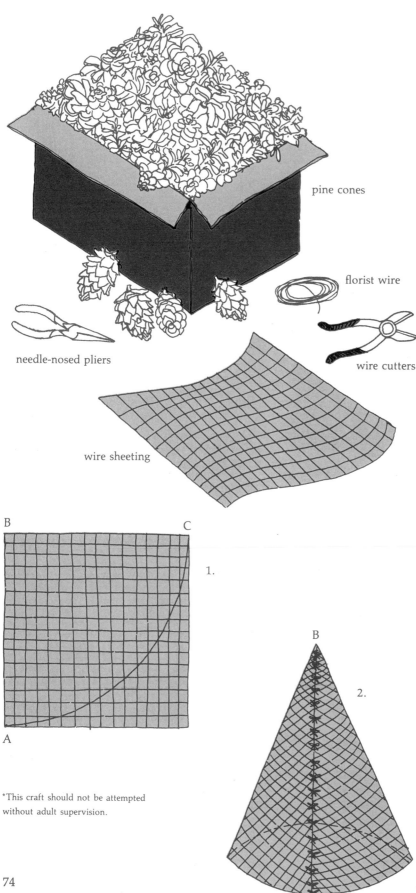

pine cones

florist wire

needle-nosed pliers

wire cutters

wire sheeting

B   C

1.

A

*This craft should not be attempted
without adult supervision.

B

2.

A C

Pine Cone Tree*

Materials:

• pine cones of various sizes and
types (A large grocery sack of cones
will complete a tree.) (If pine cones
are not readily available in your
location, check older cemeteries. The
grounds are usually littered with a
wide variety of cones.)

• florist wire (#20 gauge) (Florist
wire is available in both spools and
precut lengths at craft shops; buy the
precut lengths if you are able to
obtain them.)

• wire sheeting (Although chicken
wire will work, the ideal base for
this project is sheeting with a 1/4
inch grid, somewhat heavier in
gauge than chicken wire. This is
available at most hardware stores or
lumber yards.)

• wire cutters

• needle-nosed pliers

1—Begin with a 14 by 14 inch square
of wire sheeting. If the lower left
hand corner is point A, and the
upper left hand corner is point B,
and the upper right hand corner is
point C, imagine an arc running
from point A to point C. With wire
cutters, cut along that imaginary arc
from points A to C.

2—Take the irregular triangle you
have just cut and pull points A and
C together to form a cone shape.
Join points A and C with a piece of
florist wire. Continue lacing the two
sides together until the cone is rigid
and able to stand alone. Check the
bottom of the cone. Trim off the
sharp edges left from cutting the arc.
You may also want to fold in
sections of the bottom with pliers.
The cone should sit squarely on a
table top.

74

3—Sort your pine cones into various sizes. (Set the tinest aside for later use.) You will want to begin with smaller pine cones at the top of the tree. As you work downward, increase the size of the cones, using the largest at the bottom. If you were not able to obtain precut lengths of florist wire, cut florist wire into eight-inch lengths. Take a length of wire and wrap it around the bottom of a smaller cone and twist. The wire should be securely attached to the pine cone with two ends hanging loose.

3.

4—Run the loose ends of florist wire through the open mesh at the top of the base. Using needle-nosed pliers, pull the pine cone against the wire mesh and twist the florist wire tightly, making sure that the pine cone is securely attached to the base.

4.

5.

5—Attach more pine cones to the top of the tree base in this fashion until you have completed a circle. Place a single cone at the top to create a crown for the tree. *Note*: care should be taken as you work with one hand inside the base of the tree; *the florist wire can be sharp*. To avoid cutting your hand, trim the florist wires after twisting them and bend the ends back away from the interior of the base.

6.

6—Continue attaching cones, using larger ones as you move downward. You may not, however, wish to work the pine cones into the base in perfect circles. Use your own discretion to achieve an interesting and varied surface. Changing the angle at which the pine cones are attached will help, as will using a variety of types of cones. When the base is covered, use those smallest cones, which were set aside earlier, to fill in gaps between larger cones. (The cones from a larch tree work best.) If tiny cones are unavailable, use wire cutters to snip off the ends of larger cones. These can be worked into the tree without wire. Artificial red berries or even tiny glass ornaments might also be used to fill in holes.

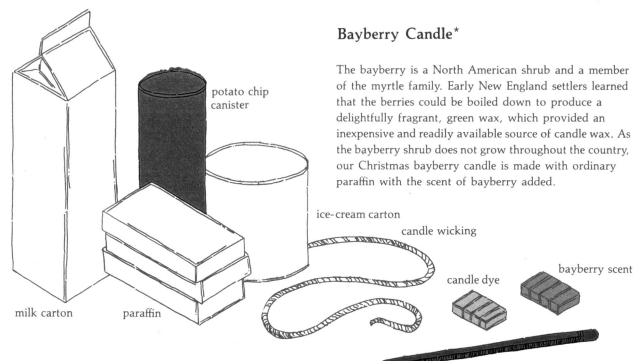

milk carton

potato chip canister

ice-cream carton

candle wicking

bayberry scent

candle dye

paraffin

Bayberry Candle*

The bayberry is a North American shrub and a member of the myrtle family. Early New England settlers learned that the berries could be boiled down to produce a delightfully fragrant, green wax, which provided an inexpensive and readily available source of candle wax. As the bayberry shrub does not grow throughout the country, our Christmas bayberry candle is made with ordinary paraffin with the scent of bayberry added.

Materials:

- paraffin (available at craft shops and some grocery stores) (Bits of old candles can also be melted down and used as a source of wax. However, some attention should be given to the colors of the old candles. A random selection may produce a muddy and unattractive color.)

- candle wicking (available at craft shops)

- milk carton (quart) or potato chip canister for use as a candle mold (Any rigid-sided container that can be easily peeled away can be used as a mold. The round, cardboard ice-cream cartons, either in pint or quart sizes, would, for example, produce attractive and unusual candles.)

- bayberry scent (available at craft shops)

- candle dye (available at craft shops) (Color can also be produced by melting old crayons into the liquid paraffin.)

- pencil

- scissors

- masking tape

- coffee can

- double boiler or sauce pan

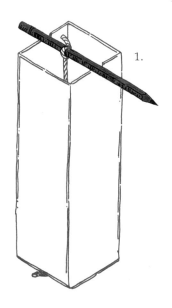

1.

1—Cut the wicking three inches longer than the candle mold. Poke a hole through the center of the bottom of the mold and pull the wick through the hole. Tie a knot in the wick at the bottom of the mold and cover the knot with masking tape to ensure that the liquid wax does not leak through the hole. On opposite sides of the top of the mold cut two small wedges in which a pencil can rest. Pull the wicking up through the mold, tying it to the pencil. Make sure that the wick runs through the center of the mold and is taut.

*This craft should not be attempted without adult supervision.

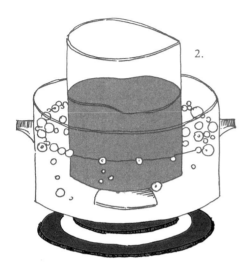

2.

2—Bend the top lip of the coffee can to form a spout. Place the paraffin in the coffee can and place the can in a double boiler. As the paraffin is highly flammable, it should be heated indirectly, that is, over boiling water. *The paraffin should not be melted directly over fire.* If a double boiler is not available, place the coffee can on a small block of wood or on a small can (such as a tuna or cat food can) in a sauce pan. Fill the pan to the level of the bottom of the coffee can with water and heat. When the paraffin is melted, add the color and bayberry scent.

3—Pour the hot wax *very slowly* into the candle mold. If the wax is poured too quickly, irregularities will form in your candle.

3.

4—Allow the wax to cool and harden. After the wax is thoroughly cooled, peel away the mold and snip the wick.

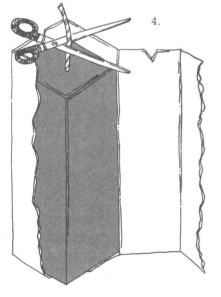

4.

5—If so desired, the candle may be decorated with holly, mistletoe, etc.

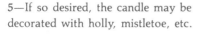

5.

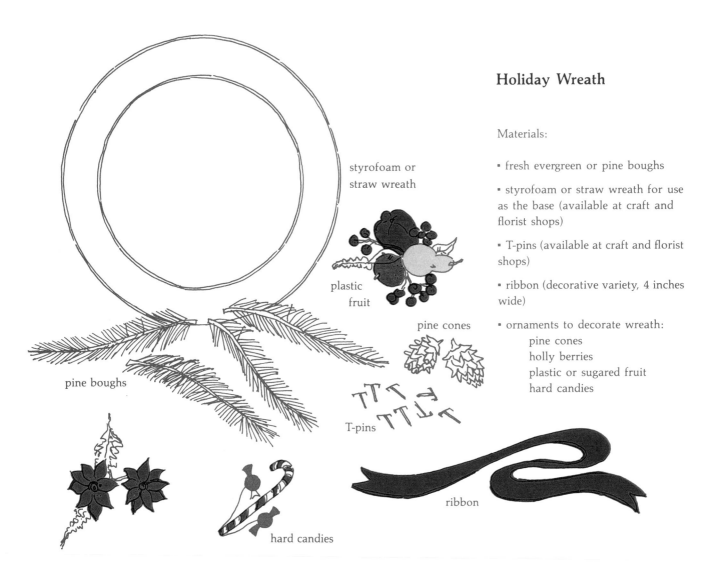

Holiday Wreath

styrofoam or
straw wreath

plastic
fruit

pine cones

pine boughs

T-pins

hard candies

ribbon

Materials:

- fresh evergreen or pine boughs

- styrofoam or straw wreath for use
as the base (available at craft and
florist shops)

- T-pins (available at craft and florist
shops)

- ribbon (decorative variety, 4 inches
wide)

- ornaments to decorate wreath:
  pine cones
  holly berries
  plastic or sugared fruit
  hard candies

1—Pin the first pine bough near the top of the wreath base. It should be pointing downward.

2—Continue to pin boughs onto the base, always working downward. (Take care to evenly distribute the evergreen boughs. Do not let the pins show.)

3—Complete the first half of the wreath in one direction. Repeat the same process with the other half until the wreath is completely covered with green.

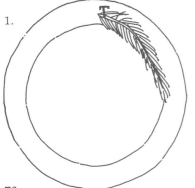

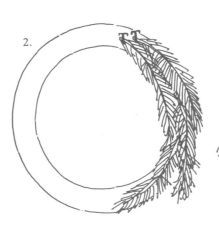

4.

4—Tie a large bow and pin this to the top of the wreath, covering the spot where the branches start. You may also wish to wrap the ribbon around the wreath, over and under the branches. (See our illustration.)

5.

5—If you choose to decorate the wreath with various ornaments, pin these to the base with T pins, taking care not to expose the pins. If ornaments are used, they should be arranged in a fairly symmetrical fashion to ensure an attractive result.

Acknowledgments

Cover: WORLD BOOK photo by Hanson Carroll
2: Granger Collection
6: Bettmann Archive
8: Culver Pictures
9: Bettmann Archive
10: Joseph Martin, Scala from Art Resource
12: Granger Collection
13: Culver Pictures
14: (Top) Bettmann Archive
(Bottom) Granger Collection
15: State of Vermont Agency of
Development and Community Affairs
16: Downtown Crossing Association, Boston
19: (Left) Granger Collection
(Right) WORLD BOOK photo
20: (Left) Bettmann Archive
(Right) Kedron Valley Inn,
South Woodstock, Vermont
22: The Bostonian Society
23: (Top) Hanson Carroll
(Bottom) Richard Benjamin, Picture Group
25: Dick Hanley, Photo Researchers
26: WORLD BOOK photo
27: Richard Hutchings, Photo Researchers
28: Tyrone Hall, Stock, Boston
29: Andrew Sachs, Art Resource
31: Hanson Carroll
32: Hanson Carroll
34: Culver Pictures

35: (Left) Eric Sanford
(Right) P. W. Grace, Photo Researchers
37: Peter Simon, Picture Group
38: WORLD BOOK photo by Neal Vance
39: Jess Smith
40: Bruce Flynn, Picture Group
42: Ellis Herwig, Stock, Boston
44: Weston S. Evans
45: Granger Collection
47: WORLD BOOK photo
48: Tom McHugh, Photo Researchers
49: Publick House, Sturbridge, Massachusetts
51: Katrina Thomas, Photo Researchers
52: Springer/Bettmann Film Archive
53: WORLD BOOK photo
54: Culver Pictures
55: Jack Spratt, Picture Group
56: Vermont Travel Division
57: First Night, Inc.
58: Tom Pantages
60: Tom Pantages
61: (Top) C. R. Benjamins, Black Star
(Bottom) Ellis Herwig, Stock, Boston
62: (Top) Downtown Crossing Association, Boston
(Bottom) Lou Jones
63: (Top) Prudential Merchants Association, Boston
(Bottom) Tom Pantages
64: Hanson Carroll